OUT OF THIS WORLD

Meet NASA Inventor Robert Hoyt and His Team's

Web-Spinning Space Spiders

www.worldbook.com

World Book, Inc.
180 North LaSalle Street
Suite 900
Chicago, Illinois 60601
USA

For information about other World Book publications, visit our website at www.worldbook.com or call 1-800-WORLDBK (967-5325).

For information about sales to schools and libraries, call 1-800-975-3250 (United States) or 1-800-837-5365 (Canada).

Library of Congress Cataloging-in-Publication Data for this volume has been applied for.

Out of This World
978-0-7166-6155-9 (set, hc.)

Web-Spinning Space Spiders
ISBN: 978-0-7166-6157-3 (hc.)
ISBN: 978-0-7166-6133-7 (pf.)

Also available as:
ISBN: 978-0-7166-6166-5 (e-book)

Writer: Jeff De La Rosa

Executive Committee

President
Jim O'Rourke

Vice President and
Editor in Chief
Paul A. Kobasa

Vice President, Finance
Donald D. Keller

Vice President, Marketing
Jean Lin

Vice President, International Sales
Maksim Rutenberg

Director, Human Resources
Bev Ecker

Editorial

Director, Print Content
Development
Tom Evans

Editor, Digital and Print Content
Development
Kendra Muntz

Managing Editor, Science
Jeff De La Rosa

Editor, Science
William D. Adams

Librarian
S. Thomas Richardson

Manager, Contracts & Compliance
(Rights & Permissions)
Loranne K. Shields

Manager, Indexing Services
David Pofelski

Administrative Assistant, Digital
and Print Content Development
Ethel Matthews

Digital

Director, Digital Content
Development
Emily Kline

Director, Digital Product
Development
Erika Meller

Digital Product Manager
Jonathan Wills

Graphics and Design

Senior Art Director
Tom Evans

Senior Visual Communications
Designer
Melanie Bender

Media Researcher
Rosalia Bledsoe

**Manufacturing/
Production**

Manufacturing Manager
Anne Fritzinger

Proofreader
Nathalie Strassheim

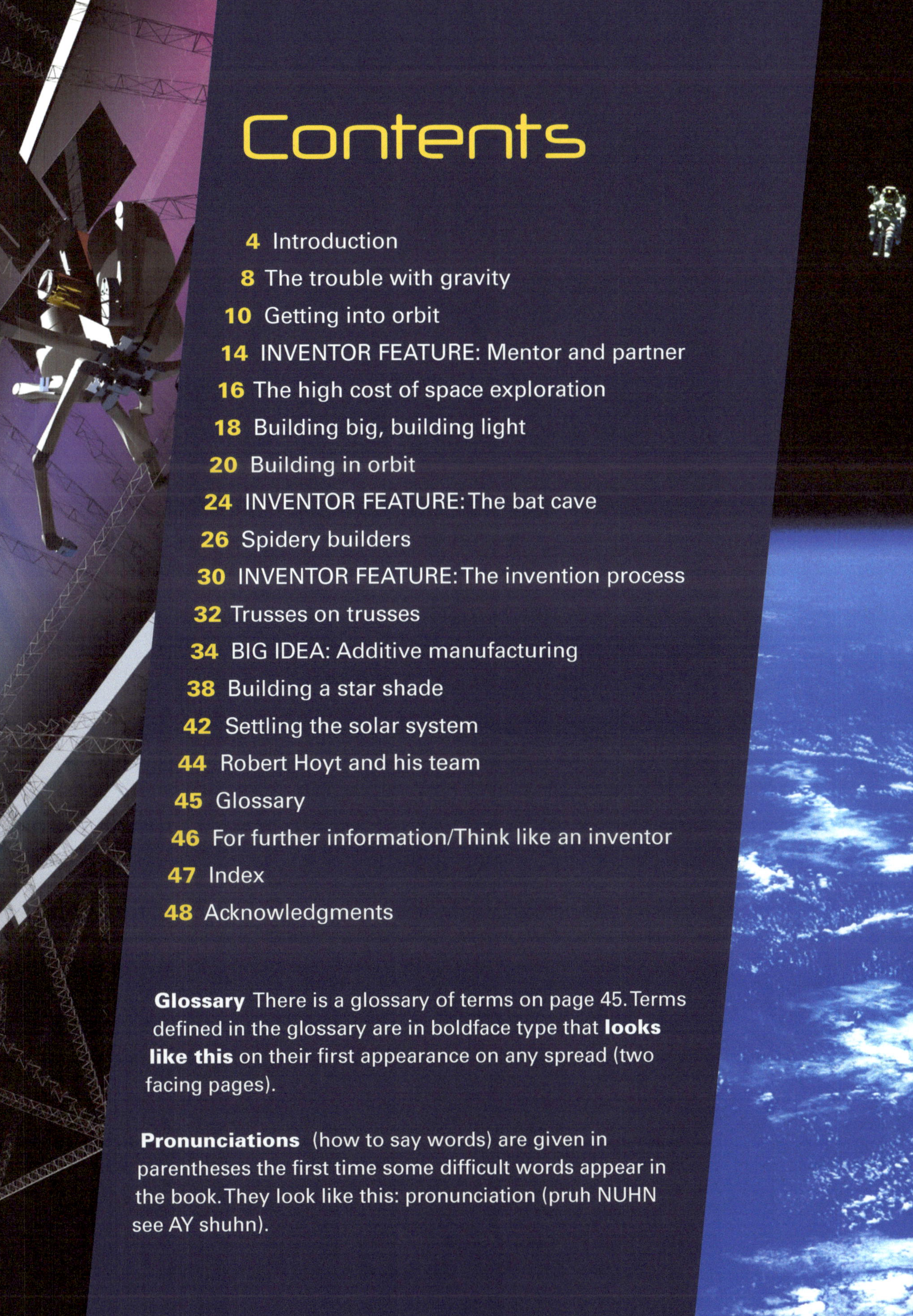

Contents

Glossary There is a glossary of terms on page 45. Terms defined in the glossary are in boldface type that **looks like this** on their first appearance on any spread (two facing pages).

Pronunciations (how to say words) are given in parentheses the first time some difficult words appear in the book. They look like this: pronunciation (pruh NUHN see AY shuhn).

Introduction

The use of spacecraft has greatly increased our knowledge of the universe around us. *Space probes* (unpiloted vehicles) have visited distant planets, moons, and other objects in our solar system. Space capsules and space stations have enabled astronauts to live and work in space. Space telescopes have peered into the most distant parts of the cosmos.

So far, most spacecraft have been fairly small. To reach space, a spacecraft must be packed into a rocket. Any large antennas or other bulky parts must be folded in such a way that they can *deploy* (spread out) when the craft reaches space. Spacecraft must also be built to withstand the stresses of launch. The extreme **acceleration** and violent shaking of a rocket launch can damage parts that are not designed or protected properly. All of these factors make it difficult and expensive to launch large spacecraft.

Larger spacecraft could improve our ability to study the universe. To get bigger craft, however, we may have to rethink not only how we design spacecraft, but where we build them. The spacecraft of the future may have to be built in space. There, free from the limitation of having to launch new craft by rocket, we could build structures nearly as big as our imaginations.

A view of the launch of the space shuttle Atlantis as it soars over the Kennedy Space Center in Florida. Large spacecraft like this are difficult and expensive to launch.

Physicist and engineer Robert Hoyt thinks he knows how. Hoyt and his team of inventors are working to develop futuristic robots that can build large structures in space. The vast, lightweight structures he envisions look something like rigid, or stiff, versions of earthbound spider webs. And not surprisingly, the robots that build them may resemble web-spinning spiders.

For their size, spiders build webs that are surprisingly large, strong, and lightweight.

Meet Robert Hoyt.

" I'm a cofounder of the space technology company Tethers Unlimited. Even as a child, I enjoyed inventing things. Now my company is developing a robotic technology to build spacecraft while in **orbit** around Earth. I call it SpiderFab. "

The NASA Innovative Advanced Concepts program. The titles in the *Out of This World* series feature projects that have won grant money from a group formed by the United States National Aeronautics and Space Administration, or NASA. The NASA Innovative Advanced Concepts program (NIAC) provides funding to teams working to develop bold new advances in space technology. You can visit NIAC's website at www.nasa.gov/niac.

The trouble with gravity

Gravity is a force of attraction between objects that have **mass.** The strength of the attraction depends in part on the mass of the object. Earth is a huge object, and its strong gravitational pull holds us and everything else tightly to its surface. Even great athletes have difficulty jumping much more than 5 feet (1.5 meters) off the ground. Meanwhile, the edge of space is some 60 miles (100 kilometers) above Earth's surface.

There is only one type of vehicle today capable of carrying spacecraft into space—a rocket. The pull of Earth's gravity can be thought of as an **acceleration.** An acceleration is something that causes a change in speed. Jump up higher and higher, and Earth's gravity will pull you back down faster and faster. That is, gravity will accelerate you toward the ground. To get you into space, a rocket has to accelerate you in the opposite direction.

Scientists measure acceleration using a unit called the *g.* At Earth's surface, gravity accelerates everything downward at 1 g. Now imagine a rocket capable of producing 3 g of acceleration—that is, three times the pull of gravity in the opposite direction. That rocket would have to burn for about 9 minutes to get a spacecraft into orbit!

"The most basic problem for any space mission is overcoming gravity." —Robert

How big is it? Sputnik

The first artificial satellite, Sputnik, shown in the photograph below, was launched in 1957. It was less than 24 inches (61 centimeters) in diameter—hardly bigger than a beach ball.

Earth has a strong gravitational pull that holds things tightly to the planet's surface. Even great athletes have difficulty jumping much more than 5 feet (1.5 meters) off the ground.

Getting into orbit

When people talk about launching a craft into space, they usually mean putting the craft in **orbit.** But what's so special about orbit?

To understand how orbit works, imagine an ordinary playground tetherball attached to a pole. If you pull the ball away from the pole and let go, it will swing back and hit the pole. Now imagine if instead of just releasing the ball, you push it gently sideways. The ball will still swing back toward the pole. But the ball's sideways motion will cause it to miss the pole and sail by. With enough sideways motion, the ball will miss the pole again and again, swinging around it in a circular path. Although it may not be obvious, the ball is still being pulled toward the pole. But to a casual observer, it merely appears to be swinging around the pole in a circle.

Now think of the tetherball as a spacecraft and the pole as Earth. The string represents Earth's gravitational pull. Given enough sideways motion, a spacecraft travels around Earth in a wide, circular path. Earth's **gravity** still pulls the craft downward, but the craft's sideways motion causes it to continually miss the planet, preventing it from crashing to the ground.

A tetherball circles its pole in much the same way that spacecraft orbit Earth. But rather than a string, it is gravity that holds spacecraft in orbit.

It takes a tremendous amount of energy to overcome gravity and get a craft into orbit. But once a craft reaches orbit, it takes relatively little energy to keep it there. Think of orbit like a stepping stone or a parking lot in space. Parked in orbit, an artificial satellite can relay telephone and Internet signals around the world. A space telescope in orbit can observe the sky above the haze of Earth's atmosphere. Astronauts can live and work aboard an orbiting space station. Space probes can even "park" in orbit on their way to other destinations in the solar system.

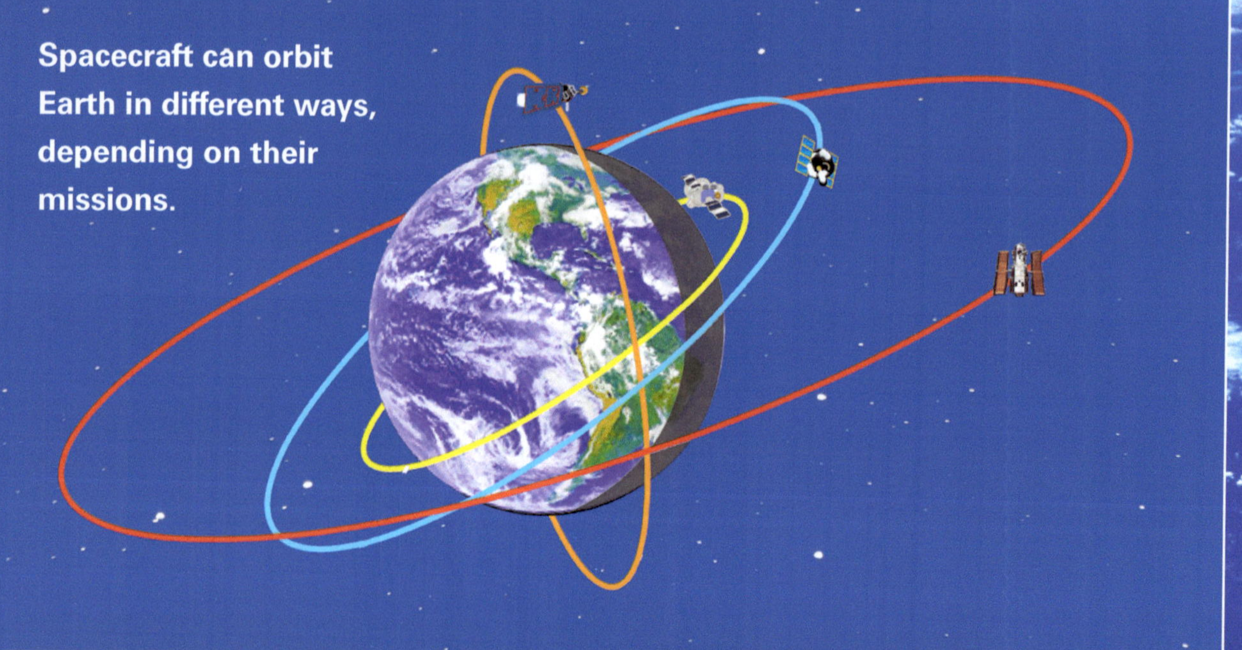
Spacecraft can orbit Earth in different ways, depending on their missions.

An astronaut works in orbit around Earth. Once something is in orbit, it takes relatively little energy to keep it there.

How big is it? Apollo

The Apollo spacecraft carried astronauts to the moon and back during the 1960's and 1970's. The entire craft was about the size of a school bus and had barely enough room for its crew of three and the equipment they needed. Yet its launch required the largest rocket ever built—the 363-foot- (111-meter-) tall Saturn V.

Apollo module

Inventor feature:

Mentor and partner

Robert L. Forward

Long before Robert Hoyt was inventing web-spinning space spiders, his interest in technology was fueled by reading science fiction. One writer in particular ended up playing a surprising role in Hoyt's career.

" One day in high school, I visited the school library and picked up a science fiction book by the author Robert L. Forward. " —Robert

The book was *The Flight of the Dragonfly* (1984), later republished under the title *Rocheworld*. It told the story of a mission by laser-powered sailcraft to visit a double planet orbiting a distant star. The story was futuristic, but Hoyt was impressed by its realistic depiction of physics. The book jacket identified the author as a physicist, in addition to being a fiction writer.

" Several years later, in graduate school, I actually got to meet Bob Forward. He was working on a space tether project. " —Robert

Space tethers are long, high-strength cables with a variety of uses in space. They can be used to link spacecraft for special maneuvers. They can even generate energy through interactions with Earth's atmosphere and magnetic field, the invisible field of magnetic influence surrounding the planet. Hoyt and Forward worked together on the project, under contract with NASA.

" A couple years later, I was finishing my Ph.D. degree. I was two weeks from graduating with no job lined up. Bob Forward and I won another contract from NASA and decided to go into business together. " —Robert

Hoyt (far left) and Forward (far right) pose with their team of inventors.

Hoyt and Forward founded a space technology company called Tethers Unlimited. Over the years, their projects expanded from tethers to include robotics, optics, solar arrays, and radios. The two men continued to work together until Forward's death in 2002.

" Bob Forward was unafraid to take on really difficult challenges and consider unconventional solutions. He had the skill and the patience to develop a practical solution from an idea someone else might have given up on. " —Robert

The high cost of space exploration

To reach **orbit,** spacecraft must overcome the pull of Earth's **gravity,** which we know to be terribly strong. A rocket accelerates a spacecraft against that pull by burning fuel and oxidizer, called **propellants.** Overcoming gravity requires a tremendous amount of propellant. Propellants can account for more than 90 percent of a rocket's weight.

Also, rockets are extremely complex vehicles. Building a rocket requires careful design and testing and plenty of precision manufacturing. Rocket launches are complicated affairs that require many highly trained people and special equipment. Further, rocket launches carry a risk of failure. A rocket that fails to launch properly can destroy millions of dollars worth of equipment and even endanger lives.

All of these factors result in an extremely high cost for launching spacecraft. In the early 2000's, the cost of launching a spacecraft by rocket could range from thousands of dollars to tens of thousands of dollars per pound or kilogram. Taking this into account, it is no wonder that the spacecraft that have been launched so far have all been relatively small and lightweight.

" So imagine you want to build a really large antenna, for example, or a big space station. Because it costs so much to launch each pound or kilogram, you need to minimize the **mass** of the system. " —Robert

How big is it? The FAST telescope

The Five-hundred-meter Aperture Spherical radio Telescope (FAST) is the world's largest single-reflector telescope. Built in a natural hollow in Guizhou Province, China, it measures about 1,600 feet (500 meters) in diameter. The largest space telescopes launched so far, by contrast, measure only a few meters or several feet in diameter.

Launching a spacecraft, such as the United States space shuttle, requires tremendous amounts of propellants and is extremely expensive.

Building big, building light

As you have read, the size of a spacecraft is limited by the weight that can be affordably launched. So, if we want to use bigger spacecraft, we will have to make them lightweight. But how do we make something bigger without making it heavier?

Engineers deal with this problem all the time, and not just in space. Take bridges, for example. A bridge must be built large enough to span a river or other obstacle. It must be strong enough to carry the weight of cars, trucks, and trains. But the bridge must also be light enough to stretch over a long distance with only a few supports.

One of the ways bridge builders solve this problem is through the use of trusses. A **truss** is a structure made up of rods or beams connected in a regular arrangement. The rods or beams are put together in such a way as to make the truss as a whole stronger.

One way to imagine a truss is to start with a ladder. A ladder has two long side rails connected by a series of horizontal rungs. Imagine that instead of being horizontal, the rungs were arranged in triangles. Now imagine that instead of two side rails, the ladder had four. The four rails are arranged in a box shape, with rungs connecting neighboring rails in a pattern of triangles. The result is a fairly simple truss.

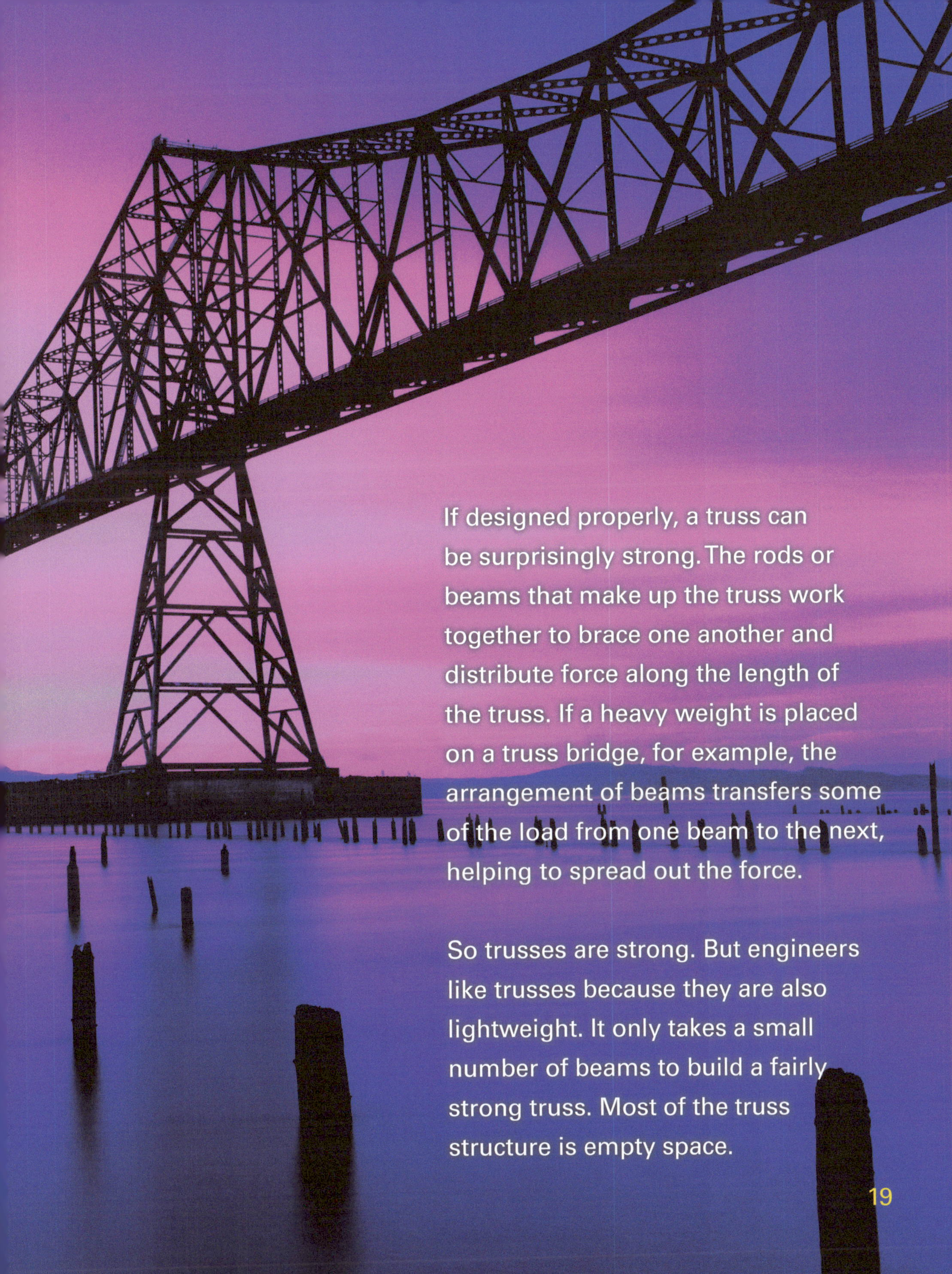

If designed properly, a truss can be surprisingly strong. The rods or beams that make up the truss work together to brace one another and distribute force along the length of the truss. If a heavy weight is placed on a truss bridge, for example, the arrangement of beams transfers some of the load from one beam to the next, helping to spread out the force.

So trusses are strong. But engineers like trusses because they are also lightweight. It only takes a small number of beams to build a fairly strong truss. Most of the truss structure is empty space.

Building in orbit

By connecting a bunch of **trusses,** engineers on Earth could fairly easily build the framework of a simple, lightweight spacecraft hundreds of feet or meters in diameter. But how would they pack such a large craft into the **payload bay** (cargo area) of a rocket? This is where Hoyt's idea becomes truly revolutionary. He and his team are not proposing to build the craft on the ground and then pack it up for launch. Instead, they want to build the craft in orbit, closer to its intended destination.

The advantages of building in orbit could be many. The first, obviously, is that the size of a spacecraft would no longer be limited by the size of a rocket's payload bay. Second, a spacecraft built in orbit would not have to be specially designed and reinforced to withstand the stresses of a rocket launch.

Finally, remember that gravity continues to pull on objects in orbit, **accelerating** them toward the ground. So objects in orbit are not really flying—they are actually falling. A spacecraft and any human inhabitants and equipment on board are all freely falling. Because they are all falling at the same rate, they do not seem to be falling in relation to one another. This special condition creates a sensation of weightlessness known as **microgravity.**

> " In orbit, you can build a craft much bigger than you could fit into a rocket. "
>
> —Robert

In this artist's conception, a SpiderFab robot assembles a giant framework of trusses in orbit.

Astronauts work to assemble the International Space Station (ISS) in orbit.

Structures built on Earth have to be built to withstand the strong gravitational pull near Earth's surface. But this ground-level pull would not affect a spacecraft being built while in orbit. Built in microgravity, a spacecraft could be larger, more lightweight, and more delicate than anything that could withstand conditions on the ground.

> " The objective is to be able to make things that are so lightweight that they probably would not be able to support themselves here on the ground. " —Robert

The International Space Station. Building in space may sound like science fiction, but Hoyt's frameworks would not be the first craft assembled in orbit. In the late 1990's and early 2000's, for example, more than a dozen nations teamed up to build and operate the International Space Station. The station provides work room and living space in orbit for a handful of astronauts. Much too big to be launched in one piece, it was assembled over time from components delivered by dozens of U.S. space shuttles and Russian rockets.

Inventor feature:

The bat cave

Even as a child, Hoyt showed a skill for engineering. A story that his father liked to tell seems to see ahead to Hoyt's grown-up challenge of making large structures fit in small spaces.

"When I was maybe 6 or 7, my father took me to work with him one day at his office in Boston. To amuse myself while I was there, I took some cardstock from the copy room. I was obsessed with the character Batman at the time, and I used the cardstock to make this fairly elaborate three-dimensional model of his lair, the Bat Cave. We had taken the bus into the city, and when my father saw what I had done he said, 'That's really cool, Rob, but how are we going to get that home?' Apparently, I replied, 'Oh no problem, Dad, it folds up!'" —Robert

The young Hoyt had designed the model to fold up somewhat like a pop-up book.

Hoyt as a child

VW-1500

Spidery builders

Here on Earth, **truss** structures are built by skilled human workers. But sending humans into space is complicated and risky. Human astronauts also require such bulky extras as air to breathe and food and water. These items add to the launch **mass** of a spacecraft, making crewed spaceflight extremely expensive.

To keep costs reasonable, Hoyt's truss structures will have to be built by robots. Engineers design robotic systems in part by considering what capabilities they will need.

"We realized that our robot needed at least three robotic limbs to be able to crawl around on a big truss structure and position itself properly. It needed two or three more robotic arms to be able to grab new parts and bond them on to the structure. Fairly quickly, the robot started looking like a spider."

—Robert

Hoyt named the technology SpiderFab. The *fab* is short for *fabrication*, another word for *building* or *making*.

Engineering imitates nature. The resemblance of Hoyt's technology to spiders and spider webs may seem surprising, but when you think about it, it makes a lot of sense. A spider's web must be lightweight enough to hang from a twig, for example, and to cover a broad area without sagging or falling apart. But it must be strong enough to trap and then hold a struggling insect. Hoyt's structures must similarly be both strong and lightweight, so it is little surprise that they resemble a spider's web. It is also unsurprising that the robots resemble spiders, as both face similar building challenges.

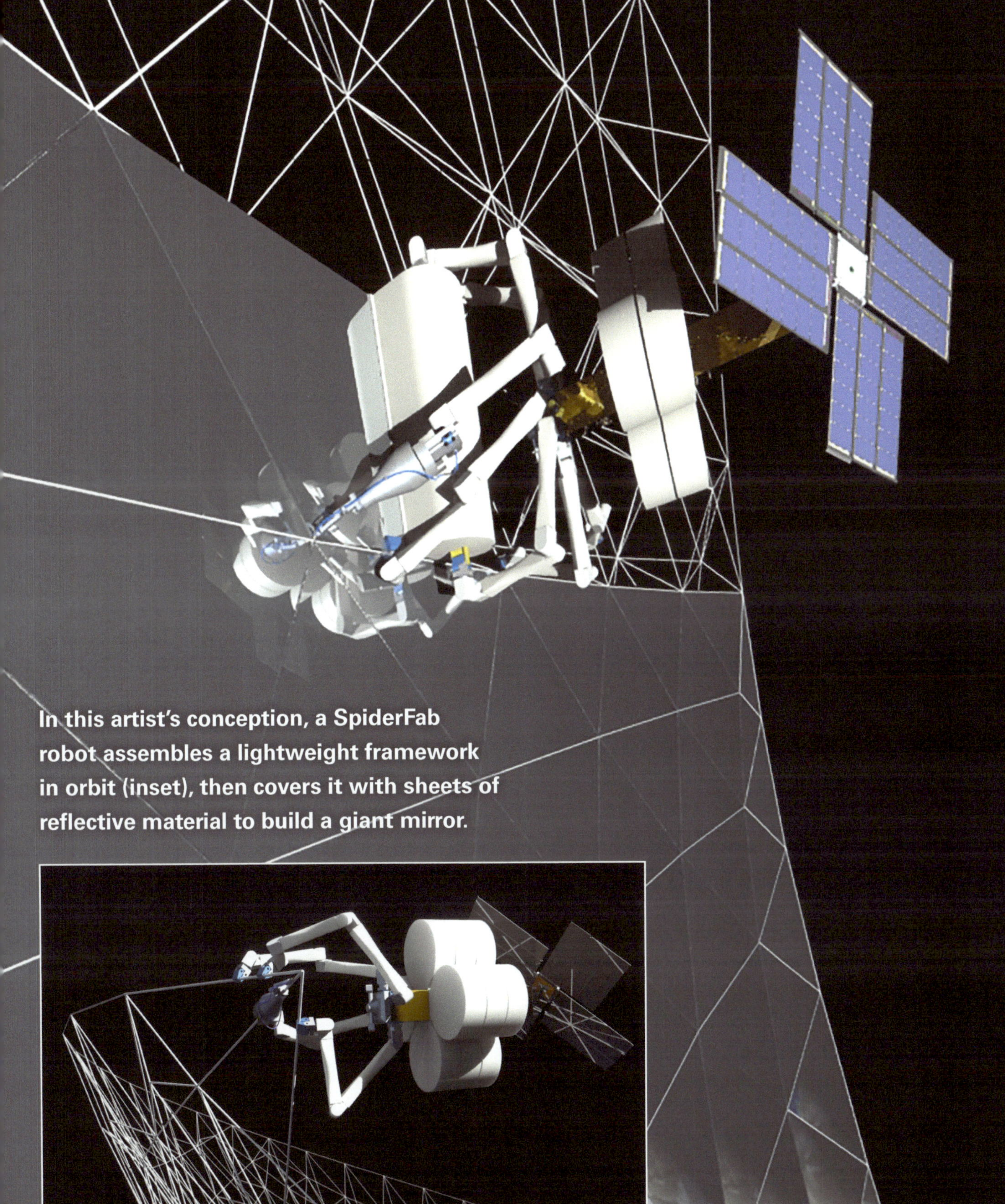

In this artist's conception, a SpiderFab robot assembles a lightweight framework in orbit (inset), then covers it with sheets of reflective material to build a giant mirror.

Meet Baxter. Hoyt's team was able to build and test a **prototype** of the robot by modifying a commercially available robot called Baxter. Baxter is typically used in factories to perform such simple tasks as packing and sorting. At about 3 feet (1 meter) tall, Baxter is safer to work with than larger industrial robots and can even be "taught" how to do a task by manipulating its arms.

> " Normally, Baxter is used for things like pulling widgets off a conveyor belt and putting them into boxes. We bought a research version that enabled us to go in and mess around with the software. " —Robert

Hoyt's team was able to configure the robot's visual system to recognize the truss parts and determine their orientation. They also taught the robot to maneuver the truss pieces into position and bond them together.

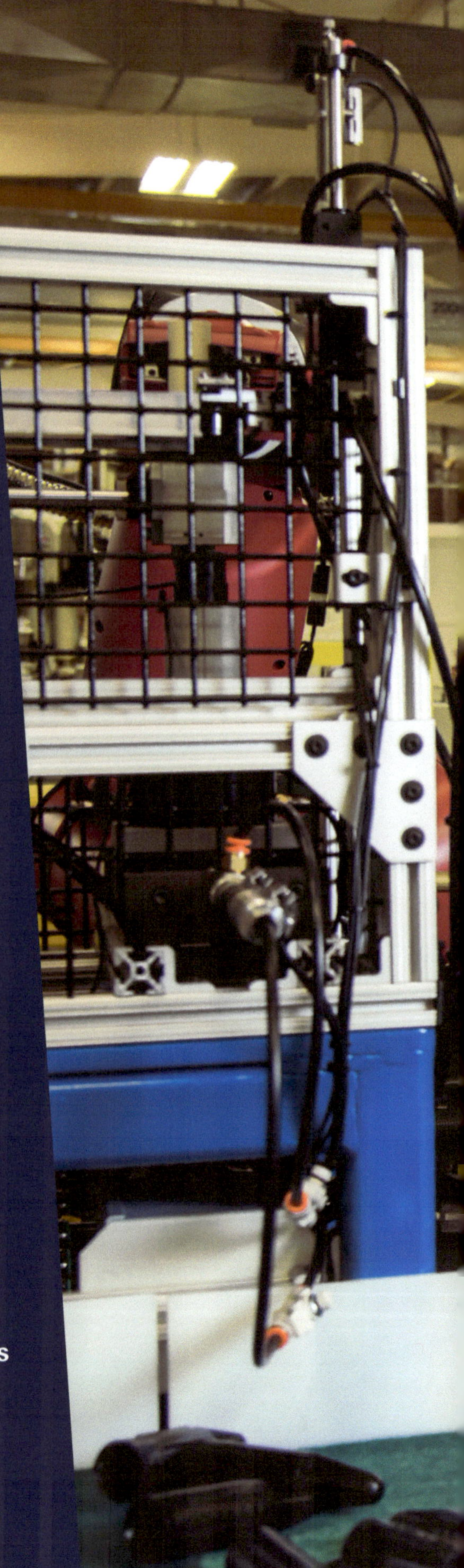

A Baxter robot at work in the laboratory. Virtual eyes on the robot's display screen help show where the robot's attention is focused.

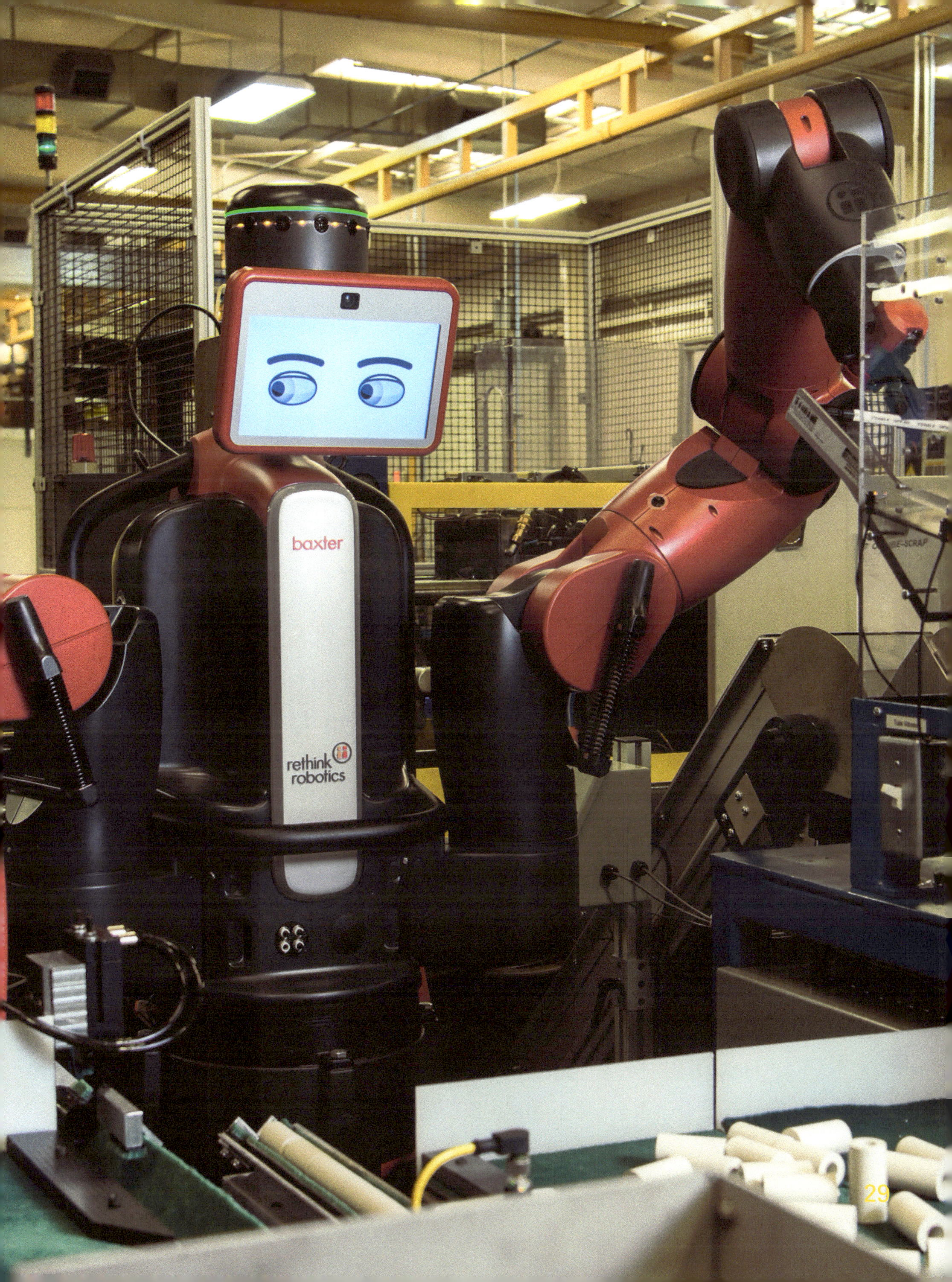
baxter
rethink
robotics

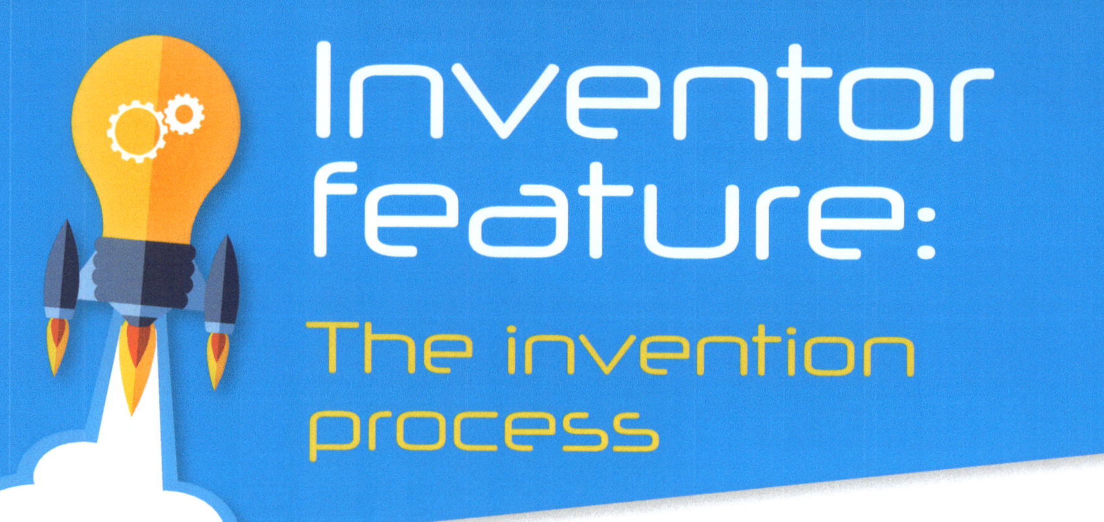

Inventor feature:

The invention process

"My team and I really like to work on big challenges in the space industry. Because of our personalities and our history, we enjoy taking unconventional approaches to trying to solve those challenges." —Robert

Space exploration is one of the most challenging of human endeavors, and giant challenges often call for daring solutions. In Hoyt's line of work, it pays to think big. Much of the hard work is done in developing the *concept*, or idea, before anything is tried in the laboratory.

"I'm kind of a crazy idea guy. I come up with the initial idea, and I have enough knowledge and skill to figure out roughly how it's going to work." —Robert

Once the idea starts to take shape, collaboration can begin. Hoyt has developed an overview of how the technology will work, but he needs help filling in the details.

"I work with a number of people who are more expert in, say, mechanical engineering or electrical engineering. By all of us working together, we can do some really cool stuff." —Robert

Eventually, work moves to the lab, where Hoyt's team can test concepts and develop prototypes.

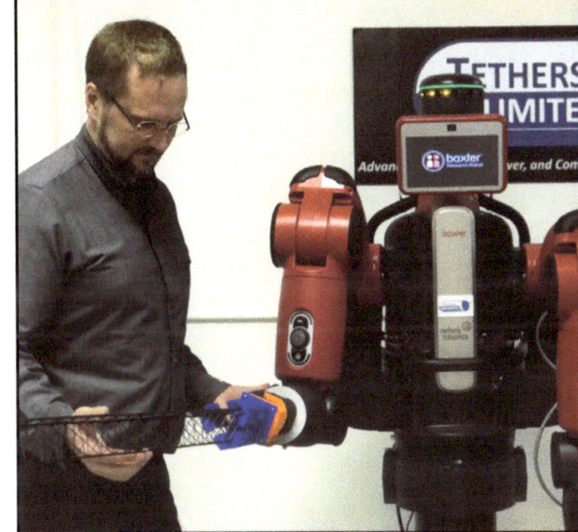

"An inventor cannot be too afraid of failure. Not every idea is going to work. But an inventor should be fearless in trying new things." —Robert

At any step in the process, an idea can fall apart. One of Hoyt's hobbies is glassblowing, and he once toyed with the idea of using glassblowing techniques to build structures in space. That idea did not turn out, but the initial challenge started him on the path to developing SpiderFab.

Hoyt has some words of advice for young people interested in becoming inventors.

"Always keep your eyes open for problems that need to be solved, and free your mind to think about potential solutions. Don't be afraid that the solutions you come up with might not work. If you keep at it, you can come up with new ideas to solve these problems." —Robert

Trusses on trusses

Hoyt's spidery builders may sound pretty amazing already. But Hoyt has at least one last trick up his sleeve. Rather than build **trusses** from simple rods or bars, Hoyt's robots will build them out of smaller trusses.

" We're building trusses out of trusses, kind of like a giant Tinkertoy® process in space. If you do that, you can get structures that are roughly 30 times more efficient by **mass** than a simple truss. " —Robert

Where will the robots get these smaller trusses from? They will make them, using another invention called the Trusselator. The Trusselator, as the name implies, is a compact mechanical device for making trusses. The machine pulls in high-performance plastic material from a spool, bending, melting, and fusing it to form a miniature truss. The device then spits out a continuous stream of truss, which the robot can cut to a needed length and assemble into a larger structure.

In this artist's conception, a SpiderFab robot assembles a huge solar panel in orbit.

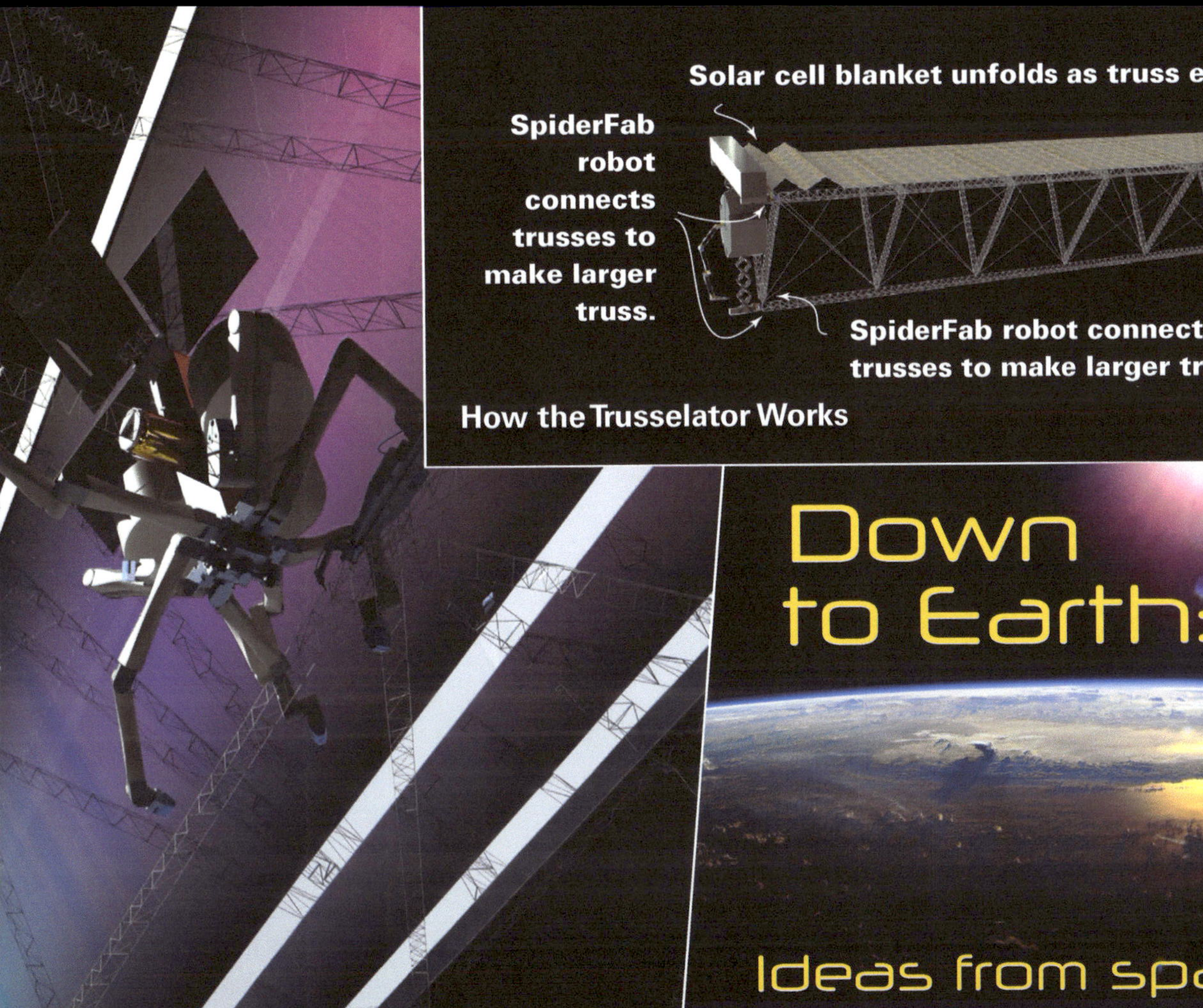

How the Trusselator Works

Down to Earth:

Ideas from space that could serve us on our planet.

Building with concrete. Here on Earth, similar robotic technology might be used to frame concrete buildings. Such buildings are made by pouring concrete over a frame of reinforcing iron bar, called rebar. In the future, spidery robots could be used to build the rebar framework, a task not that different from building SpiderFab structures in space.

Big idea: Additive manufacturing

Hoyt's Trusselator is an example of **additive manufacturing.** Additive manufacturing means using a mechanical device to build up a three-dimensional structure piece by piece. Additive manufacturing more typically makes use of a device called a **three-dimensional (3-D) printer.**

" A number of years ago, we were looking at ways to set up large antennas in space. We tested a number of unconventional ways of folding or packing them. Then about 10 years ago, 3-D printing technology really started to take off. I became intrigued with the idea of printing satellite components in orbit. " —Robert

A 3-D printer can turn a computer model into a real-life object. A computer begins the process by "slicing" the model into thin cross sections. These cross sections are sent to the 3-D printer as a series of flat images. But instead of printing the images on multiple sheets of paper, the 3-D printer prints each layer on top of the previous layer, building up a three-dimensional form.

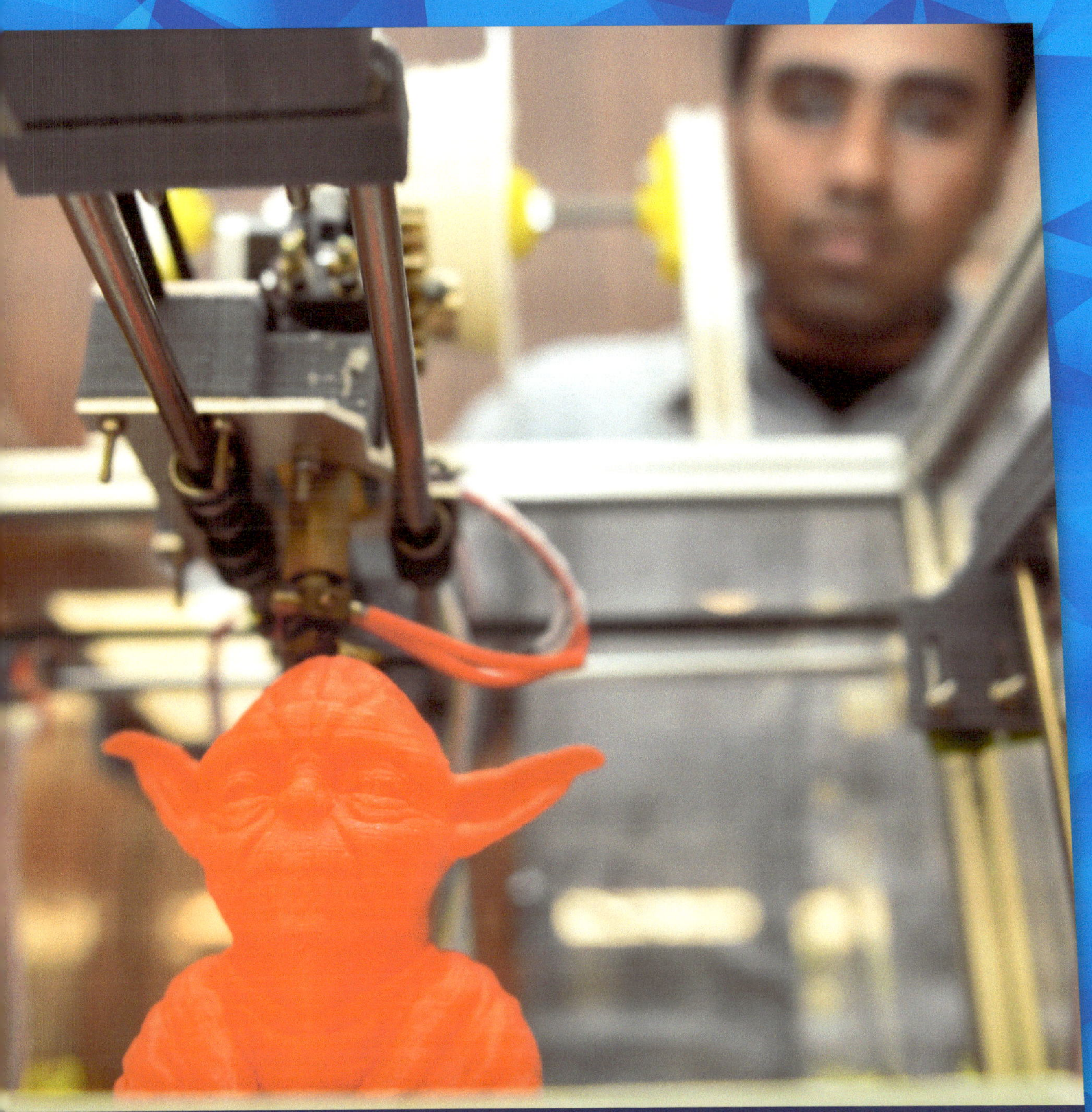

A three-dimensional (3-D) printer produces a plastic model of the character Yoda from the *Star Wars* films, building up the form layer by layer.

Big idea:
Additive manufacturing cont.

A child born with an improperly formed hand tries on a custom prosthetic hand created using three-dimensional (3-D) printing.

The earliest 3-D printers could only print plastics. Modern 3-D printers can print fully functional objects in a variety of materials including ceramics and metals.

Three-dimensional printing is increasingly common in a number of industries. Architects, for example, use 3-D printers to create models of buildings, rather than constructing the models by hand. Industrial designers and engineers often use 3-D printers in *rapid prototyping*, the quick creation of product models for testing. Industries use 3-D printers to make finished products as well. Such products include artificial limbs and specialized aircraft parts.

Additive manufacturing is particularly useful in space, where you cannot just run to the store any time you need something. In 2014, an experimental 3-D printer was installed in the International Space Station. The goal was to see if such a printer could operate under conditions of **microgravity.** Astronauts aboard the station could use it to print tools and parts they need. The longer a space mission, the more likely an unexpected need will arise. So additive manufacturing may become a part of many long-term missions, including any mission to land astronauts on Mars.

Building a star shade

The ability to build large structures in space would not just allow engineers to build bigger versions of the types of craft that have already been built. It would also enable them to do things that have never been tried before.

"One of the possible missions we looked at for this technology is the New Worlds Observer, a proposed mission to position a very large star shade in between a telescope and a distant star." —Robert

To understand the concept of a star shade, imagine trying to catch a baseball on a sunny day. It is hard to see the baseball against the sun's bright light. To catch the ball, baseball players often use one hand to shade their eyes against the sun. With the sun's light blocked, it is much easier to see the ball.

The baseball is not so different from a planet orbiting a distant star. It may be possible to build a telescope powerful enough to view the planet. But any light coming from the planet would be washed out by the much brighter light coming from its star.

The New Worlds Observer mission proposes to solve this problem by putting a giant shade in between the telescope and the star. The shade would act much like the baseball player's hand, blocking glare from the star so that the telescope can view the planet.

Compared to many types of spacecraft, a star shade seems fairly simple to build. The main challenge is that the shade has to be quite large, and it has to be in space. This sounds like a good first job for Hoyt's SpiderFab robots. Launched into **orbit** by rocket, a team of robots could construct the shade's framework of trusses. The framework could then be covered with some light-blocking material.

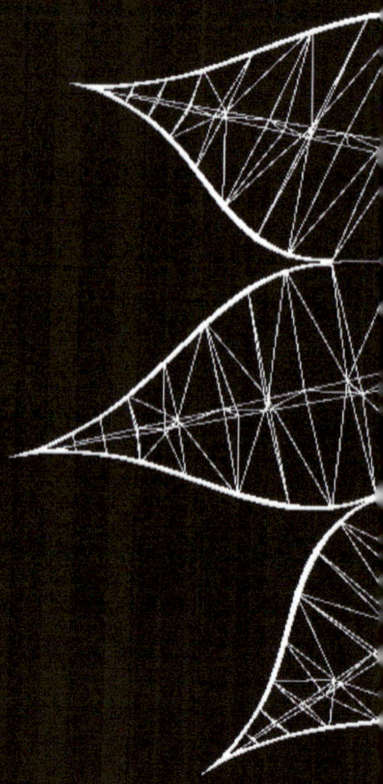

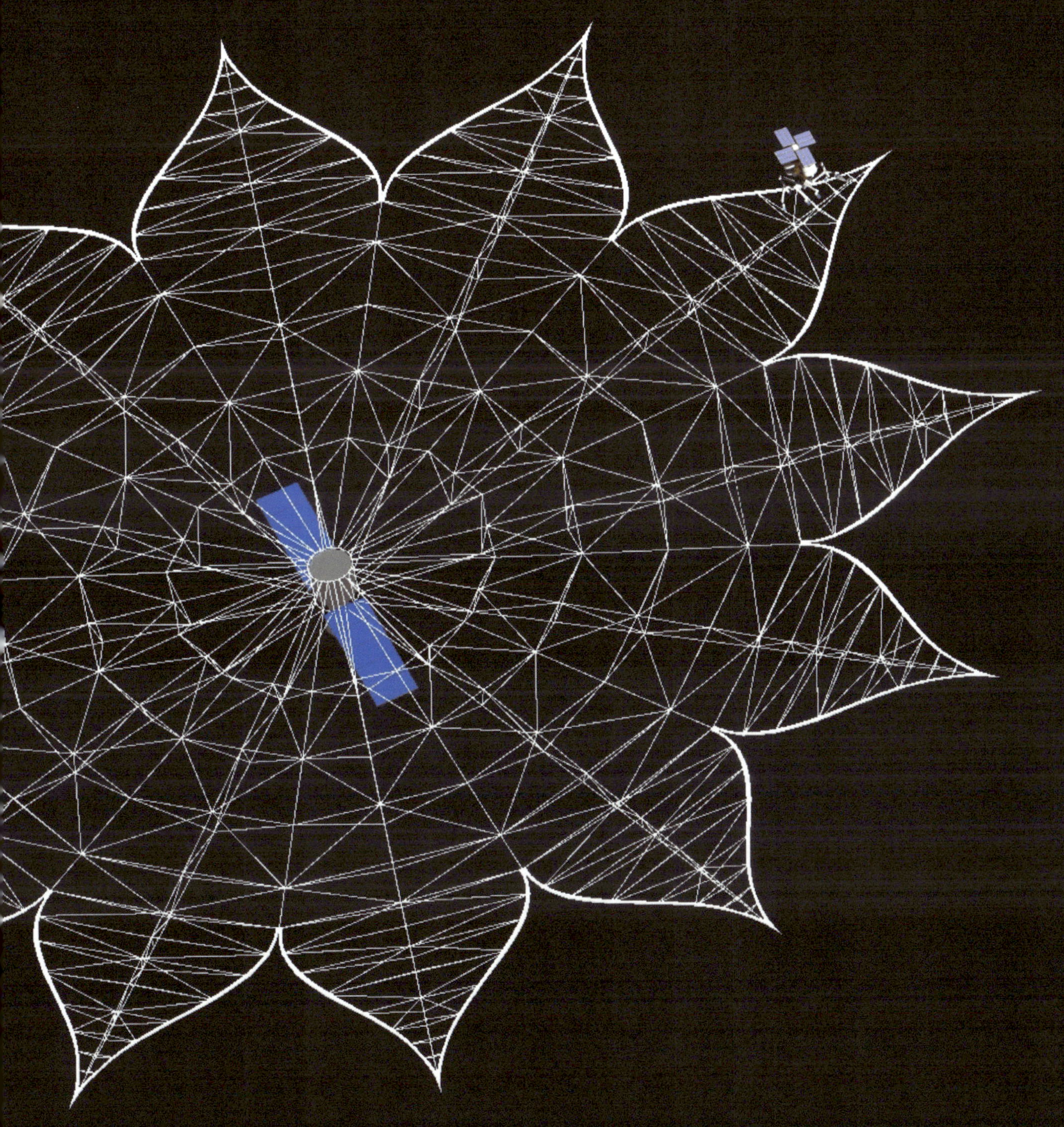

Settling the solar system

Building a giant **star shade** could be just the beginning for our web-spinning space spiders. There are plenty of areas where their ability to build big things would make a big difference in space travel. Many spacecraft, for example, get their energy from solar power. So larger solar arrays, built by SpiderFab robots, could provide more power for more ambitious missions. Larger antennas, in turn, could send back more data from such craft. But Hoyt's imagination does not end there.

"Our long-term goal is to enable the settlement of the solar system. Robots like this could be used to build the infrastructure and habitats that enable people to live in space and to develop businesses there." —Robert

It is not too difficult to imagine future generations of spidery builders assembling entire spacecraft in orbit. Such craft may one day carry astronauts to Mars and other destinations, where they may arrive to live in habitats constructed by even more robot builders.

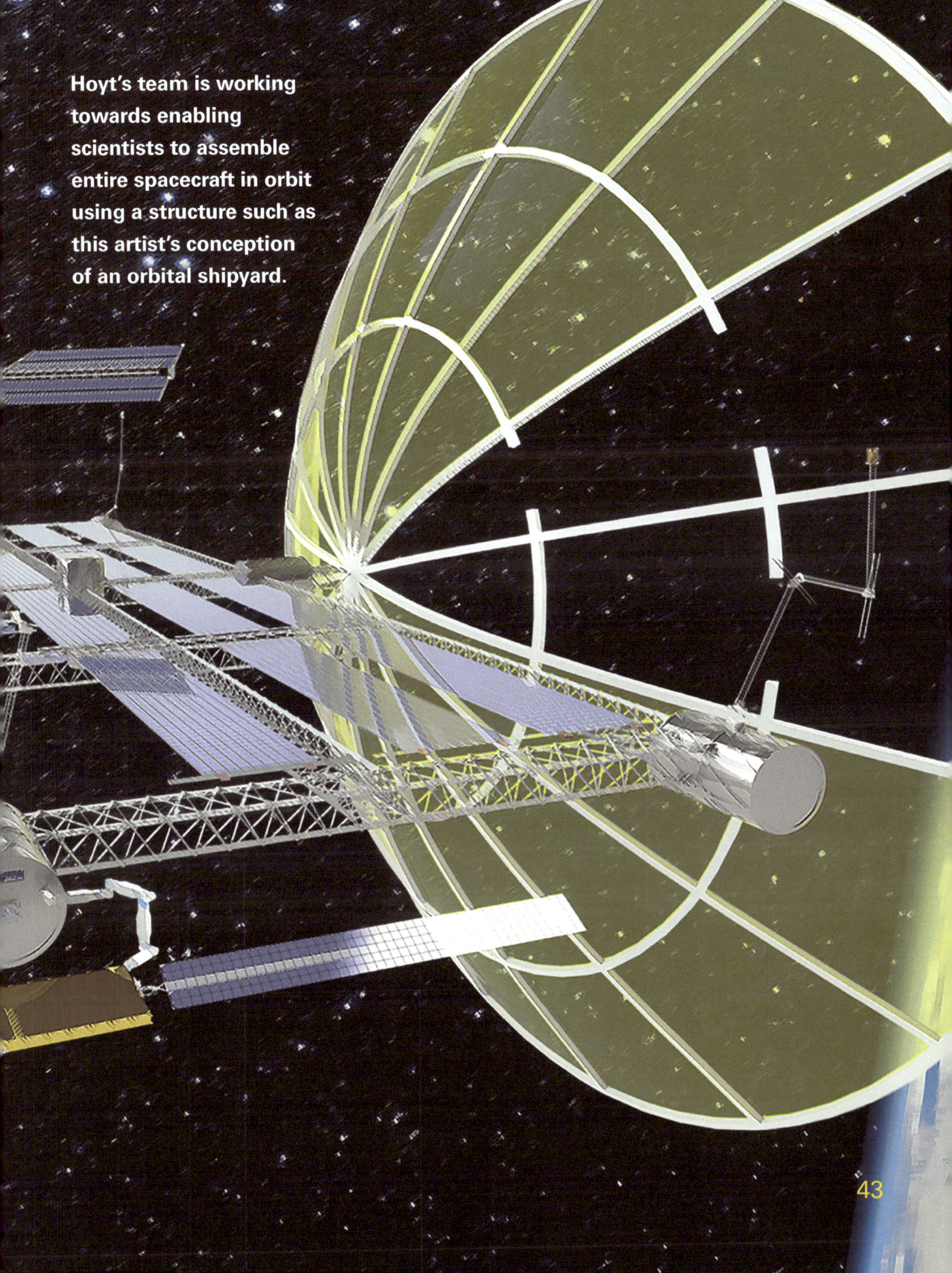

Hoyt's team is working towards enabling scientists to assemble entire spacecraft in orbit using a structure such as this artist's conception of an orbital shipyard.

Robert Hoyt and his team

Robert Hoyt and his team of engineers, scientists, and business staff at the space technology research company Tethers Unlimited, Inc.

Robert Hoyt (far right) and Jeffrey Slostad (second from left) describe TUI's SpiderFab technologies for in-space manufacturing of spacecraft to congressional staffers at the 2015 NASA Technology on the Hill event.

Glossary

acceleration (ak SEHL uh RAY shuhn) a change in the speed or direction of an object's movement.

additive manufacturing (AD uh tihv MAN yuh FAK chuhr ihng) the use of machines, such as 3-D printers, to build up something layer by layer.

gravity (GRAV uh tee) a force of attraction between objects with mass. Because of the force of gravity, an object that is near Earth falls toward the planet's surface.

mass (mas) the amount of matter in something.

microgravity (MY kroh GRAV uh Tee) a sensation of weightlessness experienced by bodies in free fall, such as people in spacecraft in orbit.

orbit (AWR biht) the condition of circling a massive object in space under the influence of the object's gravity.

payload bay (PAY lohd bay) the part of a rocket set aside for carrying cargo.

propellant (pruh PEHL uhnt) the fuel and oxidizer used to power a rocket.

prototype (PROH tuh typ) a functional experimental model of an invention.

space tether (spays teh TH uhr) a long, strong cable that can be used to connect spacecraft.

star shade (stahr shayd) a shade used to block out the light from a distant star, allowing a telescope to see any planets around the star.

three-dimensional (3-D) printer (three duh MEHN shuh nuhl PRIHN tuhr) a device for manufacturing three-dimensional objects based on a computer model.

truss (truhs) a framework of beams or other supports usually connected in a series of triangles.

For further information

Want to know more about the construction of spacecraft?
VanVoorst, Jenny Fretland. *Spacecraft.* Space Explorer. Jump!, Inc., 2016.

Want to perform your own experiments on gravity?
Solway, Andrew. *10 Experiments Your Teacher Never Told You About: Gravity.* Raintree Fusion: Physical Science. Heinemann-Raintree, 2005.

Want to learn more about trusses and building bridges?
Johmann, Carol A., Elizabeth Rieth, and Michael P. Kline. *Bridges: Amazing Structures to Design, Build & Test.* Kaleidoscope Kids. Williamson Publishing, 1999.

Think like an inventor

Look for **trusses** in the world around you. Make a list of the places you find a truss. Explain why the designer might have chosen a truss for each use.

Index

Acknowledgments

Cover	©Tethers Unlimited
4-5	NASA
6-7	© Ian Grainger, Shutterstock
8-9	© Shutterstock; © Sovfoto/Getty Images
10-11	Airman Kenna Jackson, U.S. Air Force
12-13	NASA; U.S.S.R. Academy of Sciences
14-15	© Claudia Kunin; Robert Hoyt
17	NASA/Sandra Joseph and Kevin O'Connell; Chinese Academy of Sciences
18-19	©Tom Baker, Shutterstock
20-21	©Tethers Unlimited
22-23	NASA
25	Robert Hoyt
27	©Tethers Unlimited
28-29	© Rethink Robotics, Inc.
31	©Tethers Unlimited
32-33	©Tethers Unlimited
35	© Manjunath Kiran, AFP/Getty Images
36	© Jeff Pachoud, AFP/Getty Images
38-39	© Comstock/Getty Images
40-41	©Tethers Unlimited
42-43	©Tethers Unlimited
44	©Tethers Unlimited; NASA/Joel Kowsky

www.ingramcontent.com/pod-product-compliance
Ingram Content Group UK Ltd.
Pitfield, Milton Keynes, MK11 3LW, UK
UKHW060103300726
14090UKWH00003B/371
* 9 7 8 0 7 1 6 6 6 1 3 3 7 *